Co-Conspirators

I want to give special thanks to those who helped shape this work, and gave me their busy time to make it a reality.

Mattias Ahlvin –   www.talltechtales.com

Stephanie Ellsworth –   sellsworthy.wordpress.com

Madeleine D'Este

John McConnell -   www.accelerate-motivate.com

Finish The Damn Book!

An Inspirational Guide to Writing

by Martin McConnell

Published by Gecko Print Publishing (2017)

ISBN 978-1-946938-04-6 (Paperback)

Dedication

For anyone and everyone in my life

who has ever lit a fire under my ass.

Just paying it forward.

Table of Contents

How This Book is Arranged

The original copy of *Finish the Damn Book!* was a thought experiment. It was designed to deliver motivation needed to get the average writer off their ass and working on their novel, instead of watching Netflix or playing on the Internet. The brevity of it worked to this purpose, but since I've added a bunch of content, I had to arrange it in a way that would let the reader find their inspiration in short chunks.

Any chapter should be enough to get your blood boiling before a writing session. They are short enough to finish in ten or fifteen minutes, max. So when I set out to revise this book, I kept the chapter length consistent with that idea. Each chapter is its own entity, and you can read the book from front to back, or open it to any chapter. One chapter doesn't depend on the last, so find the one that you need to kick off your writing session, and get your ass to work.

Part I: The First Draft

Packed full of all the inspirational bits and pieces you need. Finish the first draft of your novel. It is the greatest accomplishment you will make as a budding author. Finish one book, and you'll know that you can do it again. You will propel your writing confidence forward in a way that is otherwise impossible. That confidence is what makes an author.

Chapter One

How I Finished the Damn Book

I'm not a bestselling author, and outside of the bar *Chip's Daquiries* in Opelousas, Louisiana, nobody ever spots me and comes running up with a book in their hands, asking for a signature (okay, there was that one time in St. Louis). I have an okay twitter following, and I sell a few books from time to time, but I'm not making promises about turning you into a bestselling author. This book was designed to turn ordinary writers, perhaps those struggling to finish the first draft, into novelists. Sometimes your first book does well, but for most of us, it takes several novels to perfect our voice.

Despite the fact that I haven't sold a billion copies, I've never stopped sharing my advice with others, and it's always well received. My author friends don't latch on to me because they think I'm some rising star that will carry them to the top. Hell, most of their books sell better than mine. They like me because I serve as a fountain of encouragement for others, and while I might never get a seven figure contract from a publisher, I will keep writing books, and inspiring anyone that needs a kick in the ass.

You came here looking for encouragement, right? The fact that you are still reading shows that you have the thirst to become an author, no matter how scary hearing the truth may be. I'll tell you what that process takes. I've written several novels, novellas, and screenplays, and my hard drive is chock full of short stories and flash fiction pieces. Sometimes I publish them for free because I don't have time to wait on the submission process, and I always have readers prompting me for more stories. I am, as they sometimes call me, a writing machine.

And you can be too. One caveat. If you aren't serious about being a writer, then stop reading, and give this book to someone who is serious. I'm not going to blow sunshine up your ass, and tell you that there is some magic trick that will spawn manuscripts without work and determination. Save the fairy dust for Tinker-bell. Real writers have to sit their ass in a chair every day, even when they don't want to, and crank out words.

Another point. I don't care what your experience level is. Writing a novel is no different than running a marathon, getting a gold medal in an Olympic sport, or winning at a skeet shoot. It requires skill, yes, but that skill usually doesn't come from some innate talent the person was born with. It comes from years of practice. It comes from a devotion to your craft, and your goals. It comes from forcing yourself to fight the good fight, every single day. To claw for every inch.

When I started writing, I knew nothing about it, and now there is seldom a day when some random person, or a friend, or a fellow writer, doesn't make some comment about my writing, my thoughts, or the inspiration that I create. It's my daily reminder that I have to keep going, keep inspiring, and forever kick the myth that theres some magic trick that you can learn in school that will make you a better writer. There isn't. It boils down to a handful of things, which I'll discuss in this book, but the most important is words on a page.

When I started writing fiction, I had no background to fall on, no instruction booklet, and I was on a floating oil rig in the middle of the Gulf of Mexico. I literally had a word processor, the Internet, and a story. I cranked out my first draft of *The Sword of Valhalla* in 47 days. Think about that. 78,000 words, 47 days, and no, it was not November.

How did I do it? Because I didn't have any of the baggage beaten into other writer's heads. I didn't have any idea whether it would work or not, or if it would be good. To be fair, I had read some books, and tried to write some non-fiction stuff in college, but I didn't have any compass steering me wrong. Instead, I did an Internet search for something dumb like, "How do you write a novel?" Through that search, I found a website that encouraged me to finish the first draft in 100 days or less. I even had a head-start, since the story was already outlined. I did it, and dammit, you can too!

Since that first book, I've been through every newbie pitfall an author could ever hope to avoid. I went back to page one, and realized, that because I was learning from instructional writing blogs as I went, that my writing sucked. The whole book needed to be rewritten, three times. Then I learned about story structure, and after pitching it to over 100 agents, it finally dawned on me that I didn't even have a novel. I was pitching it to the wrong people, because I was too dumb to know the difference between serialized short stories and a novel. Figure that one out. I cut the sequel short, and had a lapse of "writer's block" for three years. Strike that, I let myself fail, for *three years*.

When I got back to writing, I made the decision right away. I'd failed at marriage, I hated my job, and I wasn't exactly happy that I had gone so long without writing any of the stories bouncing in my head. I was afraid to write another dud.

I vowed that I was going to commit this time, and I didn't give a damn about the consequences. It was in that moment of fury, with a little provoking from my big brother, that I became an author. I hammered out three drafts in a year, worked with them, and then scrapped the pile to start on a new book. My publisher appeared out of thin air one day, responding to a short story I had written, and that story became the Viral Trilogy.

I kept writing, and started three or four new projects. At the time, I don't even give a shit about being published. I wanted to write my stories, work with them, shape them, and do it full time. I even dropped my high-paying oilfield job to write, because I realized that it didn't matter what I wrote. Words are words, and each one is like an experience point in a role-playing game. You get enough words on paper, and you level up. Digesting learning material like blog posts, books on writing, instructions, classes; all of that shit is like power-ups and bonus items. It's all good, so do all of it, but the experience points come from actually writing.

I sat down one day, after scratching out a bunch of blog posts for a client. I was tired, and I wanted to write, but nothing new was coming into my head. I had gotten into some kind of discussion earlier in the day about writer's block, or motivation, or something of the like, and it was really bothering me. There are so many people out there who would be awesome writers if someone just stepped up and told them what to expect. If they had a boost of motivation. I didn't want to work on stories, because I wanted to put a message out. That message became this book, and I cranked out the first draft, six chapters, in a few hours. I immediately tossed it up online, and it started getting downloads. People were resonating with what I wrote. They didn't give a shit about the typos. They cared about the message.

One of my friends told me that it was just the kick in the ass he needed, and proceeded to make his word count goal for the night. He was having a rough time that day too, I suppose. I knew that I had something worth sharing, so I'm expanding it. I'm adding a bunch of extra chapters, revising or killing some chapters, and making this the best damn writing book that I can make. If you came here looking for verb suggestions, this book won't help with that. But if you need a pissed-off muse to lace your coffee with octane booster, I'm here to help. Muster up that desire, sit your ass in a chair, and...

Finish the Damn Book!

This is how you do it: you sit down and you put one word after another until it's done. It's that easy, and that hard.

-Neil Gaiman

Chapter Two

Write Something Every Day

Write every day. Simplest thing in the world, right? Except the real world is filled with bills, kids, the day-job, the spouse, the lack of spouse, peer pressure, obligations, scout meetings, PTA meetings, clubs, dinner dates, taxes, phone calls... It's a wonder we can get anything done at all, let alone writing.

Here's the hard part: forget all that bullshit. We are human beings, we're all busy, and yet we still make time for things that we really want to do. I'm floored every time an aspiring author tells me that they don't have time to write, and the next subject of discussion is binge-watching some show on Netflix. That's why you're an *aspiring*-author. I tell myself that when a person like that decides they really want to write something, they'll make time to write, instead of watching TV.

There are exactly 24 hours in every day. Most spend 8 at work, 8 asleep, 4 to 5 hours for hygiene, commuting, and basic life stuff. Then there's homework, house work, and time with the kids. We get maybe an hour or two to ourselves every day, and what do we do with it? Watch television, play games, hobby shit, or take extra time to make special meals.

I was sitting with my cousin one day, trying to convince him that a day-job isn't a bad idea while working on his real-estate stuff. I made two budgets, one for money, and one for time. It took all of five minutes, and he was floored by the results, realizing that he had way more unused time than he expected. Time he could devote to chasing his dreams, even with a day-job.

Some people have more time than others. In the oilfield, my shifts were 13 hours long, and I had no weekends. The nearest grocery store was typically half an hour from the rig, and we never really knew how long we'd be out there, so I ended up running back and forth every second or third day; another hour lost. I budgeted for 8 hours of sleep, because I had to. If anything was wrong with my equipment, the night-hand would wake me up, I'd squash whatever bug had invaded the surface system, and try to get back to sleep.

I think the reason I work so hard on my writing pursuits in the morning is a direct result of that job. I woke up an hour or two early every day, even if they got me up in the night. If there wasn't some looming disaster waiting for me, I could guarantee myself an hour or so of writing time, while eating breakfast.

I did it because I had to write. I didn't watch television, and I still don't. I saved a lot of the social media junk for five minute breaks during the day. I wrote, because I had to get words in, and I had no guaranteed time to do it. I had to take advantage of every available minute, quite literally.

Nowadays, my conversations with people about why they don't have time to write go something like this.

Them: After I get off work and help the kids with their homework, and blah, blah, blah, I just want to relax and wind down. I don't have any energy left.

Me: Then go to bed! Set your alarm clock an hour early, go to bed an hour early, and you will have an hour to write in the morning.

Them: But I can't write when I wake up.

Me: Buy a notebook, and take it with you to work. Scribble on your lunch-break.

Them: But then I can't go out to eat for lunch.

Me: Pack a lunch.

Them: But...

Am I the only person who sees where this conversation is headed? It reminds me of a conversation I had with a jobless thirty-something in a bar. He was upset. He had a degree, skills, and in his own words, he knew how to math. What was the problem? He couldn't find a job. I had to probe further, and I already finished my scribbling for the night. I think I was working on Viral Ember edits at the time. I'll give you the short version.

He got a job in his field, he loved the work, but he was getting paid the same as lesser humans who didn't have his degree or his skills, and he wanted to make more money. I told him I could make a phone call and get him a six-figure income the next day (my old boss called earlier asking if I knew anyone who was willing to work). He said the job didn't line up with his skills, and he wouldn't enjoy it. He didn't want to work even a part-time job while looking, and to be honest, he wasn't looking. He had given up, but he liked talking about having a dream job that probably doesn't exist, because every job that matched what he wanted was confronted with another deficiency that suddenly became a deal-breaker.

Writer's do the same thing, or I should say wannabe-writers. They don't really want to write, but they envision how nice it would be to have their name on a bestseller. If you aren't willing to do the work, then just don't do it, but don't kid yourself. Writers are weird. We have an addiction to keystrokes and ink scratches. We *need* to write, or we'll go insane. Addicts have their daily bump, alcoholics need their booze, and we need our words. Find me on a night when I haven't finished at least 500 words, and I'm not going to be pleasant.

But just like others, perhaps just like you, I wasn't born with this addiction, I developed it. If you don't have the addiction yet, don't take that as meaning that you aren't a writer, you just haven't gotten hooked yet. Like any drug, daily writing takes time, it has a honeymoon phase. But once you get in the habit, you'll be a rabid addict, just like the rest of us.

It started out so innocently, from my first attempts at comics as a kid, to some non-fiction and philosophical books that I never finished in my early twenties, to a screenplay I wrote after college, to my first novel based on another comic. Then my brother lit a fire under my ass one night to either get published, or he would steal my book, and publish it himself. I started writing again, and I wrote every day, almost. I tried to write everyday. I found myself thinking about my story every time I lit a cigarette. I told people about my characters when I went out. By the time I scratched out three novels in 2015, I was hopelessly addicted. I can no longer not write. It didn't happen immediately, but hooking yourself on writing is like getting sucked into a television show, or tempting fate by trying crack. You do it every day, and love it every day, until you need it every day. Then you're a writer.

Instead of telling your friends that you have to get home to watch the new episode of whatever, you tell them that you need to get home to write. Your free minutes become writing minutes. A person like that doesn't make excuses why they can't write, they make excuses why they can't do anything else, because they need their writing time.

You make time for the things you love. You make time for things that are important. If your show, or your game, or your social media interactions take priority over your writing time, then you'll never finish the damn book. Sorry.

The good news, is that you can find this mindset inside yourself. You can make writing a priority. I use fear, the fear that if I stop writing, for even one day, that the habit I've worked so hard for will disappear.

A little pep talk sometimes works too. Whatever it takes to get your ass in a chair. Type one word, then a sentence, then another. Once the rhythm starts, it's easy to maintain.

Do writing sprints, force yourself into that chair, and write crap if you have to, until the words come.

You must stay drunk on writing
so reality cannot destroy you.

-Ray Bradbury

Chapter Three

Start Today, Right Now

If you haven't started yet, start right now. Already started on your novel? Start again. Took a day off? A week? a year? You guessed it. Start, right now.

If you are reading this chapter on your computer, then open up a word processor in the background. Now.

Reading on an e-reader? open your laptop or notebook, or bust out the typewriter, whatever. Right now.

Not at home? Get your notebook and a pen. Don't have a notebook? Find a napkin, a Post-it, a blank sheet of paper. I don't care if you're sitting on the toilet, there's a roll of paper right next to you. Okay, I might be pushing it there, but you get the point, do not start this chapter without some way of getting words into print.

Go on, I'll wait.

Okay you're back. And you better have a pen in your hand. Scribble down these words, "I will move the story forward."

The rest of this chapter will be broken into sections depending on where you are at in your story. You can skip the ones that don't apply, but by the end of this chapter, I want you to have words on a page. Okay? You promise? Alright, lets go.

Phase One: The New Story

This section is for those who don't have a story idea yet. Look around the room, the bar, or wherever you are, and find a main character. You need some inspiration. You can think later, for now you need to write. It could be anything, your coffee, for instance. I'm going to give you some prompts to get you started.

The hollow cup: Your coffee can feel the end approaching. It's not sure what will happen when it's gone, but realizes that bit by bit, it's level in the cup is draining.

The tyrant: Your pen is ready to begin it's campaign against the paper. That blank page has ruled for far too long, and it's time to turn the tide. With any luck, it will someday rule the page, forever.

The desk: Ever feel like everyone is using you to prop up their work? Unappreciated and passive, but no more. Today, the desk will be noticed, one way or another.

The don't tread on me carpet.

Those two guys on the subway burst into a fight to the death.

The guy in the next cubicle has a secret fetish.

Write. Write until you have filled up a page, and see what kind of ideas you spur up. These exercises can result in short stories, or they can spur thoughts for longer story arcs. They basically free up your mind. Even if you don't turn up anything, you've still got words down, and you can go back to brainstorming your novel.

Phase Two: I have an idea, but...

So you have an idea for a novel? Awesome. Break the page in front of you into three parts (mentally, of course, or, whatever). Label each part, the top will be "the beginning: development." Write something down about the main character. Who are they, and what do they want?

Label the next part "the middle: conflict." What happens? Is the kingdom falling into darkness because [thing happens]? Is the hero lost in the woods? Does Jessica secretly love her boss? Jot down some notes explaining why the situation is complicated.

Label the last section "the end: the resolution." The kingdom is saved or lost. The hero finds his way back, or finds a pretty damsel and decides to stay lost. Jessica shags. Whatever it is, jot it down.

Now go back through the sections again, and fill in a little more, and a little more. That's right, I think you are catching on. You just wrote an outline, and you thought it would be hard. You're so welcome.

Keep working on it, start on page one, or give yourself a pat on the back for getting some words down.

Phase Three: The Blank Page

Writer's block is bullshit. You don't have to agree with me, just agree with me. Just nod, and obey. Say it with me, "Writer's block is bullshit." There, feel better? Now write it, "Writer's block is bullshit." Make it bold, that's control-B on the computer, or run your typewriter or pen back over the letters. "Writer's block is bullshit." There's actually another chapter dedicated to this topic, because writer's block is bullshit. It's a lie, made up by best-selling authors to keep you from finishing your novel.

Now that's out of the way. Start writing your fucking story. Start anywhere, doesn't matter. Don't worry about if it's chapter one, or if you need a prologue, or any of the rest of that crap. Don't worry if you are starting too early in the story, or too late. Don't worry about writing a catchy first line. You're going to change all that bullshit when you come back to edit anyway.

So, let it go, let 'er rip, just start writing the story. Describe the main character. Describe the setting. Tell me something about your new universe that is about to be born. But write, and don't worry if it's crap. It's all crap. Don't believe me? Ask Hemingway:

The first draft of everything is shit.

This is one of those moments when you need to let the baggage of a bunch of online writers go. They aren't writing your story, you are. And you will have to revise it like fifteen times after the first draft, so fuck it. Let yourself make some mistakes, and start telling your story. Ready? Go.

Phase Four: I'm not sure what to do next

If you go back and start editing the last chapter, and call it "writing time," then I'm going to alert my letter minions, and they are going to jump off this page and attack you in your sleep. You can read one page of your previous material. Just one, and then carry on.

Check your outline. Where does the protagonist need to be headed? Now put a bunch of demons, firebombs, and critters with sharp teeth all around the poor guy, and get them moving that way.

Pantsing it? You have two options. Scribble out a quick outline, see phase 2, so that you can get some words down real quick. Or, just follow the guy or gal around for a little while. Get in their head. Give them the reigns, and see where they go for a couple pages. The second you get the opportunity, drop a safe, and get them back in line.

There is one other technique that will help. Open up a new document, and write a short bit of prose about something else happening in the world of your character at that moment. It doesn't even need to have anything to do with the story. Write down what the antagonist is up to. Come up with another character, maybe your protagonist can bump into them later.

Then come back to your story and write one sentence. Any sentence. Add something to your story. Do this daily.

Another tactic is to simply put in a note that reads "finish this later," and skip ahead to the next chapter. It's okay. I won't tell anyone.

Phase Five: Almost Done

One of my favorite sayings is this: close only counts in horseshoes and hand grenades. Don't take a break, don't slack up. Keep going. There's no time like the present. Or, in the words of one of my favorite characters in Patrick O'Brian's *Master and Commander*: "There isn't a moment to lose."

Do not fall into the trap that you can take a day or two off because you are "almost done." Many a budding novelist has failed exactly at that point. Steven Pressfield provided my favorite example in *Do The Work*. Maybe after you finish writing, you can give one of his books a shot. *Do the Work* and *The War of Art* are good ones, and both are short. He'll tell you all about the perils of "almost finishing."

Every day, every spare minute. Don't stop fighting until the fight is done. What's the classic horror trope? Oh, yeah. Turning your back on the villain because you assume he's dead.

This is a dangerous time for you. I don't care what you do after the draft, but please, please. Do not stop the writing process until you're done, or you will end up regretting it.

Back to the Story

The big take-away from this chapter? The main bullet point? It's never too soon to start putting words down, and it's never too late. Once you've started on a first draft, it's of vital importance that you work on it every single day. Making excuses, procrastinating, or putting it off is like some kind of sinister force acting against you. Pressfield calls it resistance. I never gave it a name, myself, but it is something that every writer I know experiences, including me.

The only way to overcome these distractions from writing, is to write through them. Just like in life, you earn courage by being afraid, and doing the thing you're afraid of anyway. In writing, you write, even when you don't want to. *That* is what attracts the muses.

Start where you are. Use what you have.
Do what you can.

-Arthur Ashe

Chapter Four

Don't Draft a Finished Novel

Because it's not going to happen, ever. This isn't something that a novice author wants to hear. Hell, even experienced word pros will argue with it, quoting that editing is easier if extra care is taken with the first draft. And you know what? If you are already cranking out books, and nitpicking every sentence is working for you, have at it. But have you ever tried a faster approach?

I'm going to put it plainly. Nitpicking and editing as you go will result in a tighter manuscript, that's fine. But what happens when you suddenly need to rewrite several chapters? Or worse, you have to change a major plot point. That doesn't happen to you, ever? And you can guarantee that? Fine. The rest of us aren't so lucky.

Here's an example. When I'm humping ass, I can finish a first draft of a novel (80,000 words), in as little as eight days. EIGHT! Is this a habit, no? But could I do it? Absolutely. With a good outline, two weeks is plenty of time to punch out a novel draft.

With all the time some writers spend nitpicking to decide if their story is even worth writing, I would have hashed out all of the details and made a decision, I can have a first draft, on my desk, and know exactly what it needs or doesn't need. I can evaluate it to see if it's worth pursuing, and I can move onto the next story.

The first editing pass (I usually add a month of wait time here) will be scanning for big blocks of data that need to be moved or tweaked, and taking notes. That could take a week. Then I do the block edit, and make the needed adjustments. I'm a month in (in actual working time), and I have a full manuscript, and a cohesive story. Someone averaging 200 words per day? They have two chapters beautifully written, maybe three, and a bunch of sentences that they will have to kill later, which they worked so hard for.

Now, a little note here, I'm talking about full bore writing time, with few other projects standing between me and my book. Just remember that I did exactly this, working a thirteen hour per day job. Now, let's just say I spend another month tidying sentences (2 or 3 passes), a month in beta reads, and another month making more fixes and tweaks based on peer review, to ensure that my final product matches the market.

I now have a novel, ready for querying in four months. Sure, I can play with sentences and move commas around, but the novel is fucking done, in four months! Four months averaging 200 words per day? 24,000 words. Less than a third of the first draft. I don't care how flowery your sentences are. You're a third of the way through a first draft, and I'm pitching my story to agents. Let that sink in.

How do I get done so fast? Because I'm not editing. I'm not rushing back through all of the other chapters to figure out who was wearing what, and what happened to the suitcase, and editing typos. I'm writing, and pushing the story forward. Following are a few tips to help you knock out a first draft quick.

1.   Buy a notebook. I know that it seems silly and out of date, and if you prefer opening a separate document on your computer, that's fine. Keep a chapter by chapter play book of what is happening, and what all the characters are really up to. Keep track of items, such as jackets, clothing, and other ancillary items that you might mention later. Keep a running tally on everything.

2.   If you forgot to jot something down in the notebook, and you can't remember, then guess. Yes, I realize that this puts a screw-up in your novel that must be fixed later. By the same token, if you think of something that needs to be changed, pretend that it is already changed, and move forward. Jot a note about it in your notebook, so when you go back to edit, you will know to fix it.

3. Writing time is sacred. This is your job, and even if you can only offer up an hour per day, make sure that you keep to that schedule, every day, until the book is done. Put in extra time as you get it. Writing every day will keep the story fresh in your mind, and you will lose track of less of those annoying details.

4. Don't be afraid to write badly. There are times when I'm on my fourth or fifth editing pass, come across an annoying sentence, and suddenly, I know exactly how to word it. I didn't waste hours on the previous passes trying to find the right words, I let them come to me. If it's not the final pass, then it isn't worth spending more than a couple minutes on any sentence. Sometimes if they are really frustrating me, I just cut them altogether.

5. Don't listen to the experts. As a matter of fact, don't listen blindly to me either. Temper every piece of advice that you get. If it sounds like a good idea, try it for a week. If it sounds like a shitty idea, then dump it and move on. Just smile and nod at the advice giver.

6. Do NOT doubt your talent. Even for a second. Don't give up. If you notice a fault in

your writing (and you should from time to time), then work on fixing it, but keep moving forward. This is how we grow, not by speculating, or going back to page one. We become authors by putting words on a page. Allow yourself to make mistakes as you go.

7. "That's what the editing phase is for." Anytime I catch myself making some silly mistake, or even a huge mistake, I shake it off and repeat this mantra. Any minor worry about the book. What genre does it fit into? Finish the book. Is my word count on target? Finish the book. Been using semicolons wrong all along? Finish the book. Don't have a name for that character? Finish the book. Don't fret about all those irrelevant details. Everything can be fixed with editing, and you will know better how to fix it. So, just finish the damn book.

8. Don't go back to page one, ever. Trust me on this one, okay? If you finish a chapter, and edit, and do another, and edit, and another, and back to page one, editing, you aren't ever going to finish your book. Some people are going to disagree with me, let them. But every time I've tried to write a book this way (and I

have several times in my youth), I have never managed to finish the first draft, and never realized the wonder that is editing.

The gleaning point of this chapter, is that as an author, you must be brave. You must be willing to stumble and make mistakes. Trying to cover them up is going to cost time and energy. It's going to drain your motivation, and cripple your ability to finish. It's going to let all the monsters of self doubt out of their cages to run free over your psyche, and eventually they will convince you to quit. Finish the draft, before it finishes your author career.

Fortune favors the bold.

-Latin Proverb

Chapter Five

Writer's Block is Bullshit

Inspiration is bullshit, too. I sit down everyday and write. I regularly crank out thousands of words. Why? Do I have some supernatural ability? Nope, but I like getting paid. When you job is writing, you constantly have to blast content. My clients don't care if I'm tired or sick, or I need to have my teeth cleaned. They want output, and they want it on a deadline.

I knew going into the freelancing world that it would be writing from the trenches, and it is, but I also knew that I could draft articles and PLR reports, write short stories, or dress up dull content with cute and witty commentary. I knew this because of how I write novels.

I read, edit, and sometimes completely re-write work that my clients paid for, and lost money on, so that I can turn it into something they can sell. The more I do this, the easier it is to sit down and go to work, even if the muse is taking a day off. When I started writing my first novel, I didn't know how writers did it. Through helpful daily writing quotes from a blog, I learned to make use of my time and tell the story, instead of over-thinking the process, which I'm usually terrible about.

I write everyday, all day, and when I finish with my freelance work, I concentrate on my stories and books. The stories are the good stuff. They aren't scratching your head trying to come up with a witty headline for your blog that will appease the Google gods. They aren't droning out on coffee and retyping shitty words because the original author couldn't speak English. Writing a novel? That's the fun stuff, so stop fretting, and start enjoying it.

In the last three years of writing nearly every day, I've never experienced this thing called "writer's block," though it hit me in the early days. Even though a muse does occasionally drop by and kiss me on the cheek, that's not the norm. I don't think it's ever been the norm, for any writer.

When people ask me how I come up with ideas to write about, I usually tell them what I do when I really need an idea fast. When I got my commission to write Viral Spark, it was still this humble little short story about some kid living in a shitty apartment with cool special effects. I had to turn it into a series of novellas, and fast. Here's what I did.

I ordered a pizza with extra pepperoni. I scrounged up every sci-fi DVD in my house, and I bought a case of beer. Not kidding. I set an alarm on my phone for 4am, and another one for 9am. I started drinking, binge watching science movies, and scribbling every stupid idea for a story that popped into my head. After going through the process, I can't say that I recommend the beer.

I woke up at four o'clock, went outside for a smoke, and wrote down more ideas nursed by the crazy dreams brought on by greasy pizza.

When I finally crawled into my hangover later that morning, I had pages and pages of ideas. I chose five that looked good, drank a ton of water, cleaned myself up, and went straight to Barnes & Noble to start drafting. I cranked out 8,000 words, despite the hangover. The next day I did another 6,000, and I finished the first draft on day three. Three days, from brainstorming to done, and the only real inspiration was a headache that refused to go away.

Joking aside, I think my real inspiration was finding someone that liked my stories. This is why I'm an advocate of show and tell. Somehow, in that moment, the years of hard work leading up to it was enough to inspire not only that novella series, but everything I've written since.

My outline for Viral Spark consisted of a two-page spread, with four headlines across the top: the best ideas from dozens that I had written in the night. Under each headline was a story arc. "Virus hacking people, virus becomes self-aware, virus helps Robert." That kind of thing. An outline doesn't have to be some elaborately detailed list with a fancy indentation scheme. I filled in some of the blank space with a few extra details, and went to work.

Steven Pressfield calls it resistance. I call it lack of drive or motivation. But it *can* be overcome. The blockages are real, they happen, but the stigma of this being some kind of wipe that arrests the mind of a writer from the outside is a cruel fabrication. It gives us an excuse not to write. We don't have to feel bad if we throw up our hands and say, "writer's block." We can sleep easy, because some force beyond our control has denied us the ability to create.

I've never, ever, believed in that sack of crap. I'm here to drop it on your doorstep and set fire to it, if that's what it takes. Writer's block doesn't come from some mythical outside force. It's that age-old mind trick of your inner dialogue talking you out of something because it involves work.

The fact that it's a lie isn't a pass, and I'm sure you didn't read this chapter to hear me make fun of it. Blockages are a real problem, but they aren't crippling, and they aren't random.

Blockages can come from things like a death in the family, loss of a friend, a break-up, or maybe someone that pissed you off earlier. They come from being tired or dehydrated. They come from eating too much junk food. They come from a resounding sound byte cycling through your mind, clogging up all the bandwidth.

If you're tired. Sit down. Open the document. Tell yourself that you are going to write one sentence and then go to sleep. That first sentence might spark another, but write one sentence, and consider it a win. Your first victory against the dreaded writer's block. The battle that turned the tide forever.

All it takes is one sentence. I've had days where I literally added three words to my manuscript, and then went to bed.

Can't get work done where you are? Move. Take your notebook or laptop, and go to a coffee shop, a bookstore, the park, a museum, a library. Anywhere but where you are, and grab some caffeine on the way.

Train with treats. Grab a bag of candy, and eat exactly one piece after each paragraph, or each page, or whatever. Any kind of positive reinforcement will work for this, but my favorite is SweetTarts.

Follow the main character. Don't worry about the excess crap words. Just picture your main character in your head, and write what he or she is doing. They might stumble around for a while, but once the words are flowing, they tend to create more words, and before you know it, the story is moving again.

Work on something else for a while. Write one sentence on your story, and then draft a piece of flash fiction about something else. You can write it about writer's block. You can start a journal. You can write up a news article and post it on Facebook. Whatever. Then get back to your story.

Let me tell you what writer's block really is. It's the monster under a child's bed. The novice writer is the child, terrified to go to sleep, and no night light or teddy bear is going to save you. You fight off the monster by standing up to it. Toss off the covers and shout, "do something." When you call it out, you'll realize that it can't hurt you, because it isn't even real. You'll take a stand, and come up with your own creative ways to fight it off. You'll be writing, just to annoy it, the way it has annoyed you. It's your way of telling the monster that you aren't afraid. Adapt that mindset, and Writer's block will crawl back behind the screen, and you can get your work done.

Inaction breeds doubt and fear.
Action breeds confidence and courage.

-Dale Carnegie

Chapter Six

No, I Don't Need a Day Off

It's not okay to not get your words in. When you are drafting a novel, one single day missed can sometimes be recovered from, but too often, it turns from one day without writing into two, into a week, a month, and then forever. I wrote this book because all too often, I see this happen to otherwise good writers. By the time they come back to finish the book, they've forgotten the story, and have to re-read the whole damn thing to get caught up again. Their brain figures out how much work it's going to be, and internal dialogue derails their efforts.

Anytime someone tells me that it's okay that I missed a day, I might force a smile and a nod, but on the inside I want to chew them out. I want to rip into them about exactly how okay it is not. I've left too many books behind in this fashion. After your rack up two or three half-novels, you'll know what I'm talking about. It's never okay to miss a day of writing, unless it can't be avoided, especially when you are drafting a novel.

I've gotten to the point now where I will refuse to miss a day out of terror. Trepidation rings through every bone in my body, and every soft tissue attached, that if I miss just one day of writing, I won't finish the book. I told my brother once that I draft fast because I have to. If I pick up any new project, writing or otherwise, and don't finish it in 90 days, then it'll never get done. I lose interest. I lose my passion. You might have a longer attention span than I do, but you should still beware.

I remember being at my mother's house one day. I often stay there, because it's close enough to my property to serve as a base camp, where I can work on my professional writing gig in-between trips. I was upset. I don't remember what happened earlier that day because it doesn't matter, and it wasn't as important as writing.

I said something about taking the rest of the day off, and relaxing with my favorite video game: Kerbal Space Program. I was exhausted from the fast-paced events of the morning (probably scrambling to finish something for a new client), and I felt spent.

The previous chapter is about writer's block being a load of donkey dung, and it is, but that doesn't mean that we, as writers, don't get bogged down from time to time. It doesn't matter whether you are logging trees, or working a cash register, there are days when you finish your normal daytime stuff, you want to call the day "over," and just go to sleep. I needed to refresh.

She said something to me about how I'd been working too hard. How I had been staying up until after midnight every night and then jumping out of bed at six in the morning. How she never saw me without my laptop. "You need to take a break," she said.

Now, I love my mother, don't get me wrong, but when she sounds like one of those stupid voices in my head, telling me to slow down and take a break, I tell it like it is. I said something, half tongue-in-cheek, like "That's not what I need to hear today. Or ever. I never need to hear that it's okay to take a break."

As a continuation of the sarcastic communication, she said, "Well fine then, stop sitting around and get your butt back to work! Is that what you want to hear?"

I smiled. That was exactly what I wanted to hear. I still needed to recharge my batteries, so I set an alarm on my phone for one hour. I played my game until the alarm went off, and then took a shower, my second of the day. I changed clothes, laced up my boots, grabbed my laptop, and disappeared into the little writing den. And I didn't come out until I had 500 words down.

I don't even remember what I was working on at this point. It could have been an editing pass for the horror story (in which case I wrote bits of flash fiction between chapters), or some bit of work that I needed to finish.

They say that writers have thick skin. In essence, if you ever want your words to actually be read, then you need to have thick skin. Reviews suck. Criticisms suck. But those sucky bits are necessary for growth and development. We need feedback. But that thick skin serves another purpose. The people around us can help our motivation.

Online, I get it. These people don't live with me, they don't know me, and I don't have to tell them how many hours per day I spend slacking off. My closest writer friends only see a word count, and a stream of motivational energy.

Even so, those closest to you, your friends and family, can have the strongest pull on your motivation, and they always seem to be pulling you away from your target, not pushing you toward it. A long time ago, I started wondering if coaches being soft on me was part of the reason that I sucked at everything. I started pushing myself in high school, and I improved, quickly.

I think that was when my inner coach entered the equation. If you think this book is harsh, I should let *that* guy write a chapter. All that voice does is yell at me, constantly, every day, and I love that voice. Anytime I need a quick bit of motivation, I conjure up that cross between Al Pacino and Joe Pesci, to yell at me in a way that inspires. It goes something like this:

"You've been sitting there on your ass for thirty fucking minutes. If you would have started thirty minutes ago..."

I'll spare you the rest, I need to keep my blood pressure in check at the moment. But those little pep talks stir up energy, they seem to create it. They call into existence a fireball that burns in my muscles, boiling my blood and setting me in motion. *That* is what I need to hear.

Say what you want about some pseudo-psychoanalysis of my character, only one important thing matters. That fictional coach in my head is never, ever, going to tell me that I need to take a break.

I guess I have to sleep sometime (gosh, life is so inconvenient), but until I've done what I need for the day, I'm not letting go of any momentum that I've built up. When I'm writing a novel, coach is always turned on. I'm too scared of having to scrap another book to turn him off. My novel infects every aspect of me. Every cigarette is a meditation on how the next scene is going to go, every break at work a reflection on the overall scope of my story. If you really want to see me pissed off, interrupt me when I'm sitting down to work on a first draft.

I suppose I should pad this with the fact that anger isn't a particularly useful emotion, and I've learned to harness it in a certain way that enhances my focus. I'm not even sure I can call it anger, because it doesn't really come with any of the baggage. It's more like fury, just something to get my blood running, to get me moving. There are other (probably more productive) ways to accomplish the same thing.

In the end, just make sure that you know all of the consequences that come with "taking a break for a day or two." An inner coach can help with that. Ensuring that you've scheduled your writing time can help with it. If you know that you are going to be tired during your normal time slot, then it's important to do some prep work. Think about your story, and where you want to go. Do some jumping-jacks before sitting down to write. Get some extra-strong coffee. Whatever it takes. And if you don't want to take a break, don't let anyone convince you that you should.

Don't succumb to excuses. Go back to the job of making the corrections and forming the habits that will make your goal possible.

-Vince Lombardi

Chapter Seven

Ragged Out and Writing

Tonight is, perhaps, the most perfect opportunity for me to write this chapter. When it comes to blockages, resistance, or whatever you want to call that unholy force that keeps us from getting words on paper, it comes in several varieties. Most all of them boil down, ultimately, to one solution, and the very existence of this chapter stands as proof of that.

Last night, I got about 3 hours of sleep. Not sure about your habits, but I'm not used to that. I couldn't fall asleep, I couldn't stay asleep, and I had to get up early to help out with a promotion campaign for a friend, who also didn't sleep much last night.

I did manage to fit in a nap, but on top of the regular promotion, I've been working around the clock to build a couple of new social platforms, and promotion day means engagements on social media. I probably sent over 200 tweets, posts, replies and messages today, maybe over 300. Most of it has not been copy-paste. It wears you down.

At this moment, I feel like going to sleep. The fires are almost all put out. Everything can wait until tomorrow. But what the hell kind of inspiration would I be if I let that stop me, especially in the middle of adding content to this book? I came back to part one, and decided to add this chapter, because I'm getting my 500 words tonight, and there isn't anything else I want to work on, at least as far as my personal writing projects. This is it.

Now, I'm going to be straight with you. It wasn't easy to start typing. Every time I went to start, I allowed myself to get distracted. I probably killed an hour letting my mind get the better of me. Telling me that I needed to concentrate on this or that instead of writing. Making me believe that I didn't know what to write about. Opening the folder was hard. Opening the document was harder. Putting my fingers on the keys and hitting go? That was the breaking point.

The same goes for all blocks when it comes to writing. It's a rare thing, especially in 2017, to have no physical way of getting words down. If you can speak, you can write. But saying it, or thinking about it, is different than actually doing it. I'm still yawning, even through this paragraph. Exhaustion has taken it's toll, but I write.

Once I slid everything else to the side, and told myself, "no more Internet until you get another chapter done," in that instant, something hit, and I knew I had to write this chapter. I don't care if I need to reformat some things to make it fit. Doesn't matter. Tonight was the perfect example of overcoming this monster that people call writer's block. I'm fighting the monster right now, with every word, and every keystroke.

I went to the table of contents, to put in a chapter title, and the monster fought back. Three or four minutes later I realized that I was on the defensive again. I hammered out a few words that looked something like a chapter title, and moved on. I scrolled down, made a new chapter heading page, and then I was golden. The first paragraph was a hard won victory. I defeated the monster, or so I thought.

This small bout of enthusiasm made me feel comfortable enough to check another social media message, and again I was drawn away from my writing. It was only for a couple minutes, but it may as well have been a day. Not everyone has two or three hours in the night. We have jobs. We have lives. We have dishes and dirty laundry.

I went back to the document, and continued writing. Once again, the words were flowing. Once again, I had control. Once again, the monster backed off. At each sentence break, and every paragraph break, I have an idea that will destroy my chain of keystrokes. They come in the form of tiny voices of reason:

"I should make a blog post, right now."

"I should rename the chapter title."

"I wonder if so-and-so messaged me back. I hope everything is alright with him."

"Oh man, I forgot to check my other email today."

These voices are the demons of doubt and frustration. They are the destroyers of motivation. They will be the end of your writing if you allow them to be. I'm even skeptical about checking the word count so far, just to see where I'm at. It will only take a second, right? No, I must go on. I must finish what I started, and I don't even know if the chapter will convey the meaning that I intended. I don't know if it will resonate with the reader. I don't know if it will help. I'm not sure what quote to use in closing. I don't even know if these words will ever see the light of day, yet I continue to hammer away at the keys. The story moves forward, not back.

I'm in a position where aside from correcting typos, I'm encouraged to leave this chapter exactly as it stands. This is the writing process. Everyday. All the time. It's hammering away at the keys. It's ignoring those little voices telling you why you need to stop typing, and look at something else. As Steven Pressfield puts it, it's "doing the work."

You keep writing, always forward, never back, and at this point I don't care how many words are in this chapter. I've done what I set out to do. I hope this rambling fills a purpose. I hope it inspires you, or at least lets you know that you are not alone. You too, can do the work, turn off the world, and finish the damn book.

> *Writing is most of all an exercise in*
> *determination.*

-Tom Clancy

Part II: Post Draft

The process of becoming an author begins with the first sentence. The process of publishing begins once the first draft is complete. Publishing requires a totally different mindset than drafting, and by the time you get through the hell to come, you'll realize that writing was the fun part.

Chapter Eight

Start the Next Book

Okay, the book is written, the draft is done, make sure you celebrate. Buy yourself something nice, or gorge on chocolate, or whatever. Enjoy it for a minute. Then, when the party is officially over, start again. After you get done cleaning flip-cups and chocolate wrappers, it's time to get back to work.

Probably the best piece of advice I ever gleaned from another author was shortly after I finished my first novel. I had been stuck in editing land for months. Work on the novel, work on the novel. What I should have done was stick it on the shelf for a while. Going over anything repeatedly is going to burn you out, even your wonderful masterpiece.

But if you take a break from your book, then what? The first draft is done, so you no longer need to worry about finishing. The story is downloaded from your brain to the computer. It's safe, mostly.

This is probably a good time to inject that you should have a back-up or two. Save the file to a CD, or at least an external hard drive or memory stick. If you can, print out a physical copy. Don't think about it, just do it.

Your novel needs some time to rest. If you go straight to editing, the story is still going to be fresh in your mind, and you won't be able to catch cavernous gaping plot-holes.

The secret sauce, is to start the next book. Start plotting, start drafting, and start writing little stories about your new host of characters. Do research, and keep notes about some new world building. Invent vivid characters with rich histories and strong personalities. Just like you did in the first book.

External influence can help you with that. And if you aren't in the middle of drafting a novel while reading this, you might consider joining an accountability group to help. My favorite can be found at writingchallenge.org.

Get on the forums, and meet other authors. Form a local group. Join a local group. If the group goal is to keep everyone writing, then being part of a club can be beneficial. Just be sure that everyone is there to write. Not to chit-chat or gossip. NaNoWriMo is another wonderful group.

The wisdom that you gained from finishing the first novel is still as fresh in your mind as the story. Use it. This is your chance to get ahead for the next story, and concentrate on all the deficient areas of the last one.

My first novel was a historical fiction piece, so naturally I didn't do enough research. Looking back on the whole thing, I don't think that it's possible to do enough research before starting a historical fiction novel, but whatever.

Maybe it was how to place a comma, the best way to use dialogue tags, or some other grammatical nuance that kept tripping you up. Maybe you were unsure about your story arc. Whatever the case, now is the time for all those distracting little voices to be put to work. You remember? All the voices telling you that you couldn't write a novel because...fill in the blank. Write them down, and make sure that they don't have a place in your next book.

Maybe you aren't ready to draft another novel yet. That's okay, I've got a whole list of writer stuff that you can work on while your manuscript is curing on the bookshelf.

Write Short Stories

Or better yet, write some flash fiction. I have a Facebook page waiting for all the little 200-300 word stories that you want to dump and share. Maybe they will spread, and some people will start following your writing. The kind of people that might want to buy your novel once it's in print, for instance.

You can also submit your work to magazines, newspapers, local columns, or whatever. Some of those markets pay. And if you are getting money for your stories, that will look really good on a query letter. Especially if you win an award or two in the process.

Submissions also give you practice pitching your work to publishers. 1000 words isn't a novel, but a rejected query can be devastating all the same, and you'll learn a lot through the process. Give it a shot.

I'm going to throw some tips on submission into the appendices by the way. Wink.

Start Blogging

You don't have to run your own website (though it probably wouldn't be a bad idea to start tinkering with WordPress), but just put something out there. Sites like Medium and Wattpad are a good place to start.

You can write some stories, and give people a chance to read them. You can set up your own Blogger account, just for your stories. Understand that once it's published to the web, you can't really pitch it to most sites, but it's still a wonderful way to spread the word about your writing, and begin building a following at the same time.

People love free stuff, and storytelling is hard to sell. So giving some little pieces away, and engaging with an audience, is pretty much the only way to find readers. As a bonus, some of them might want to try a beta sample of your book later on, and they can give you feedback. Testing your book on a small audience will give you a good feel about what people think of your writing. Start building that audience.

Read Writing Blogs

And writing books. And all things writing. Start a daily dictionary search for new words to expand your vocabulary. Visit sites like Writers-Digest to get new insights about publishing, marketing, and writing tips. Scour the Internet for new tricks that can help your story.

I'll tell you that I learned more in six months studying what other writers and novelists had to say then I ever did in school. This is 2017. The web can be used for posting funny memes, selfies, and pictures of cats, or you can use it to enhance your knowledge of the craft.

Read

Pick a book in your genre and give it a read. Try out new authors. Experiment with writing short bits of prose in another style.

If you don't think that reading is crucial to your success as a writer, believe me, I know where you are coming from. But at the same time, you are asking other people to read your work, why aren't you reading too? It's hard to advocate reading when you aren't a reader. I'm not going to harp on this, because most of this book's audience consists of heavy readers, but for the few of you out there who aren't, these little breaks are the perfect opportunity to give another author a chance.

My favorite thing to do is cherry pick stories from Amazon's short-reads section. I can find a dozen or so stories in the thirty minute category for free. Love them or hate them, if you are only out thirty minutes, then who cares? It's not a huge time investment, and it will expose you to dozens or hundreds of new voices. Try to learn from each one, especially the bad ones. They are shining examples of what not to do in your book.

If you don't have time to read, you don't have the time (or the tools) to write.

-Steven King

Chapter Nine

Build a Social Platform, NOW

If you think that it isn't part of being an author, you're wrong. If you think your publisher isn't going to care, you're delusional. If you think it shouldn't matter, then you're just so darned cute!

Welcome to the 21st century! The world of social media is here to stay, so it's time to get your shit together, and get with the program.

One of the biggest misconceptions about that big publishing deal that everyone wants, is that somehow you will become an instant overnight success. All the tears from any negative feedback can be wiped away with the hundred dollar bills from that fat advance check. People think that the publishing house is going to hire some genius publicist like Ryan Holiday, and your book is going to explode in a flash of green bills that rain down from the heavens.

Nope. Not even close.

First flaw in this line of thinking, is that publishers nowadays, and agents for that matter, are going to check out your social profile. They're going to search your name on Google before they make a decision on getting back to you. Not saying that it'll kill your chances, but 10,000 twitter followers looks a hell of a lot better than a search that returns nothing.

Don't know anything about social media? Too bad, neither do the rest of us. But you get on there for a little while every day and figure it out. Play the follow game on twitter, and then nix anyone who isn't following you back a week later. Sign up for Instagram, or Flickr, or whatever platform looks tolerable to you. I've lost track of how many social media platforms I am a member of. I forget to check half of them most days. But now that the draft is chilling on the shelf, you have some time to look around.

I know how you feel. Believe me, I know. I didn't want to sign up for Facebook for the longest time, and there are days when I still regret the decision. I had to be badgered for months before I finally got a Twitter account. I resisted Instagram forever. In fact, I'm still timid, most days, about signing up for the next big procrastination station.

But you know what? It pays off. If you can figure out how to interact on even one platform in a way that builds a following, then you're golden. My twitter account exploded fast, despite my resistance. Actually, it was probably because of my initial repulsion that I grew my following. I wasn't having fun on there. I was only using the stupid thing to build a platform. I followed and unfollowed people meticulously.

I decided early on that I wasn't going to engage in any tactics that would get my account flagged, so I made a simple rule. You don't follow back within a week, and I drop you like a bad habit. I stayed a fan to a few major accounts, just to keep up appearances.

The funny thing is, the people that followed me back started engaging me. I interacted with them, liked them, and got involved in a writing group. Have never looked back, and now, without my artificial meandering, my account has over 6,000 followers, and continues to grow a little every day, all on it's own.

It was one day, while making a map of my social media accounts, that it finally dawned on me. If even one of these accounts hits big, it's going to infect the rest of them, and I can leverage that overflow to grow my other accounts.

Nobody nowadays has one social media profile. Everybody out there who depends on media, advertising, or any kind of publicity (and that includes authors) has multiple accounts. There are some they play on more, and others they turn over to bots or publicists.

Another downfall of thinking that landing a book deal will be the final chapter in your life as an author, is that you are going to have to promote. You have to get out and show your face at book signings, conventions, meet-ups, and all this other public nonsense. Most of it will be promoting your book online. When people like your book, they are going to want to check you out on social media as well. They have friends on social media. They have book clubs on social media. Do not piss them off by failing to make an appearance, okay?

I know that you want to be busy on your next book, but it's not okay to hide from the world and let the publisher handle it. They'll get you on the shelf. They'll put out the press release. But that isn't going to magically make your book a bestseller. *You* have to promote it.

Now, before you get on your high horse and attempt to chastise this author for being "small time" and not understanding, I'll inform you that I am actually close friends with a lot of traditionally published authors. Jaded authors. One of them recently had his contract expire, and happily pulled his books to self publish them.

This is how it works. A publisher tosses a bunch of money out for the book, if you get that far. If they don't make that money back in a given amount of time, then your book is a flop, and you'll carry that black eye around forever.

Don't believe me? Fine. Go to Google and search "Confessions of a bestselling author." See what comes up. You don't even need to bother with the bestseller links, concentrate on the mid-lists. If you can't build some momentum for your book, then that will be your future. And if you ever self publish, well. There you go.

I'm not saying any of this to scare you. If you land a decent publishing house, they're going to give you a boost. They'll help you promote your book, a little. But you are the author. If you want it to sell, then you need to do the leg work. And it starts with building an audience ahead of time. The easiest way to do that, is to learn social media, figure it out, become an expert. I can't give you a simple list of exactly how to do that, there isn't room in the book, and I learn new tricks every day. Most of the time it doesn't even feel like tricks. It's just interacting long enough that you figure out what spreads and what doesn't.

When it comes to promotion, there are some very talented authors out there worth reading, like Chris Fox and Ryan Holiday. I've listed a couple of their books in Appendix B. Look them up, but at the end of the day, you will be the one building the platform.

Men strike out their permanent characters; or have those characters struck into them.

-Patrick O'Brian

Chapter Ten

Write Fast, Publish Slow

So, this question has been finding its way into my inbox a lot lately. Authors coming to me and saying "I finished my book, how do I publish it?" My response in person is pretty nice, and I get to the point gradually. I'm not going to do that here, so put on your rubber skin, and get ready for a dose of truth.

If you are asking this question, then you aren't ready to publish your book.

There. I said it. The nice version of this advice is, "take your time," but it amounts to the same thing. I'm not saying this to be a jerk, and I'm not trying to discourage anyone from publishing a book, but there's a reason this question shows up repeatedly on Quora, Reddit, the AW forums, and everywhere else. It's answered time and again, and nobody ever listens to the best advice. It's like they've already decided to go with CS or with a vanity press, and they are simply looking for permission. This is NOT how you publish books, people.

To illustrate the point, I'm going to discuss the traditional publishing model a little bit. I'm not saying that you need to go this route. There's nothing wrong with self-publishing, but for heaven's sake, do it right. There's many reasons that publishers don't publish and push every single book that shows up in their inbox, and I won't discuss all of the details of that, but here's the publishing process in a nutshell (update: the Chicago Style Manual contains a great chapter on the publishing process):

Author finishes first draft, edits meticulously, sends copies to friends for review, edits some more, etc. Finally, they print out their masterpiece and give it a hug, taking in the scent of fresh paper. It's ready, finally.

Author scours the Internet, as well as a couple of books designed for this purpose, and compiles a list of *literary agents* that might be interested in their "baby." (Yes, you must call the MS your baby, this is a writing requirement, lol) The writer then drafts a *query letter*, and perfects it. This takes longer than an editing pass on the book. They adapt the letter to each agent, and start pitching.

After many, many form rejections, and hopefully a couple insightful comments, an agent reads the query letter, thinks "this is the next number one bestseller," and requests a full manuscript for review. This process will iterate a couple of times also, most likely, but eventually, in a perfect world, one of those manuscripts wows the agent, and the die is cast. Here comes the writing career!

The agent advises the author to get their shit together and build a social profile, and possibly sends some notes back about fixing the novel. Meanwhile, she's busy working her ass off, doing market research, putting together a proposal, and fixing the original query so that publishers will read it. She might call in a few favors as well.

Everything tidied up, the agent pitches to publishers, gets an offer for the book, and helps the author understand the contract details. Agent's do a *lot* of work. I'm not defending them, I'm just saying.

Publisher buys the book, assigns their own editor to read it, and sends a list of more fixes back to the author with a deadline. Publisher spends a fuck-ton of money on an advertising program, cover design, interior design, etc. Sometimes they will hire a publicist. Basically, there are a bunch of people working to get your book on the shelves and well received, even if it looks like they aren't doing much. They're investing money in your words. Oh, and you get an advance check, which is typically broken into two or three installments that are paid over time.

Publisher tallies up all the money that they spent on your book, the release eventually comes, and the clock starts. If your book earns back all of the money they spent, it's a success.

If it doesn't, it's a flop. That's the single criteria for book sales. It either made the money back, or it didn't, in x number of months.

That's pretty much it. I left out a few details, but that's the process. As you can see, it's hardly "print it out, and push the publish button." Even if you plan on self-publishing, I highly recommend trying your luck at this process at least once. At the very least, learn how publishers do it, and emulate their model.

There's a lot involved with getting a book to market. Professional edits are important, and expensive. Find a good editor and give them some money. Want to design your own cover? Go to the bookstore and do research. Look up design elements that will help your book stand out on a shelf in a good way, or fish it out to a professional. Interior formatting is a thing, as is a normal block-size for the paperback. 5x8 and 6x9 are pretty safe for most novels. (Hey, *this* book is 5x8, haha!)

When you get your book back from the editor, edit it again. Send it out to someone who is great at finding typos. Test your cover design on social media with your audience. Learn to write a press release, and send them out. Contact bloggers, and beg them to advertise your book. Send them free copies to review, and send some to book reviewers as well. Prepare a social media campaign, set up some book signings (in collaboration with other local authors where possible), give out branded bookmarks and stickers. If possible, reach out to local film-makers. In other words, all that shit that you are passing on by going self-pub is going to fall on you, in addition to the normal promotional stuff. If you can spring for it, hire a publicist.

Oh yeah. Get a website, and set up social media accounts. That goes for indies and trade-published authors alike. You need to put your name out there. Your audience should be able to find you. Start building an email list. Leverage reviews to get more reviews. Hustle, hustle, hustle. Worn out yet? Now do it all over.

I said it in another chapter. Writing is the fun part. Publication and promotion will leave you wanting to rip your hair out. But if you want your book to sell, you need to do it. This is why it's so important to study the inner workings of the publishing industry. I spent months after writing my first novel learning how to pitch, and how the whole process worked. I read books by other authors, reached out to other authors for advice, and spent countless hours trying to learn every facet. It was quite an education, and every part of the process is important.

Now, do you have to do all of this? No. You can log into KDP right now and stick whatever you want on Amazon's Kindle program. But if you didn't do the work, then it's going to show. If you are short on funds, you can get an Amazon branded ISBN for free or cheap, I forget what the current product offer is. You can hire freelancers on Upwork to do some of the design stuff for cheap. There's a lot of options out there, but please, learn the process. You're book deserves to at least have a chance, right?

And remember. If your book was awesome yesterday, it'll still be awesome tomorrow. I encourage everyone to speed through the first draft, but as the revision process takes on a life of it's own, you should be slowing down, and coming up with a plan. Publishing is easy. Hell, you can post your whole book on a Google drive, and toss a link on social media. Bam. Published. When you decide how you want your publication process to go, and what *you* are going to do to drive sales, then you're ready. You need to have very clear goals for your book before you hit the publish button, traditional or self-pub. Trust me, you'll save yourself a lot of heartache in the long run if you take your time with this step.

And while you are working on this, start writing the next book.

By failing to prepare, you are preparing to fail.

-Benjamin Franklin

Chapter Eleven

Edit Fast

Everyone has their own system of editing. There are some common themes amongst most authors, but the universal truth is that it takes longer to edit then to write. Another common theme is that the editing system is refined and optimized with every book. I have trouble remembering how many books I've written at this point, and most will never see the light of day, because I only have time to edit the best ones.

I'm going to walk you through my editing process, because I think it's a nice average of all the different methods that I've heard of. You will likely find some things that you like and some that you don't. Like every other chapter in this book, it's a pretty short read, and my hope is that it will give you a compass to follow for your own book.

Don't take this as any kind of doctrine, or anything like that. It's simply an example, here for you to reference when you begin the editing process. If I didn't think there was something to be gained from this chapter, believe me, I wouldn't have included it.

Time Between Edits

There needs to be sufficient time for your brain to rest between editing passes. If you jump straight from one edit to the next, then you are going to get confused by your own words. You'll miss redundancies between chapters, and gaping plot holes.

I generally recommend at least 14 days between consecutive passes through a novel, though for some people with better memory, 30 days might be more appropriate. The goal is to forget enough of the story details that you can look on the manuscript with fresh eyes.

Doing this will ensure that the next time you page through your story, you will be able to see everything in sequence, and won't be left wondering, "did I already say that in an earlier chapter?"

First Pass

This isn't really an edit so much as a read-through. I check my story notebook to make certain there are enough blank pages left, and I read through my story. Straight through it. I do exactly what a reader would do, except while reading, I'm also taking notes.

When something stands out, a plot hole, or just a minor error, I don't bother fixing it (unless it's super easy to fix). I might tidy up some typos as I go, but I try my best not to edit. I want to see the story from the reader's eyes. I want to experience the pacing and tempo, the crescendos and decrescendos. I want to see the big picture.

So I read, and make lots of notes about changes that need to be made, what different characters are wearing, what they look like, if I gave them time to eat, etc. Any little details that seem important get noted.

Block Edit

Don't ask me why I call it a block edit, the name just sounded appropriate, and I ran with it. This is probably the biggest pain in the neck of the whole editing process. I fix all of the big mistakes that I found in the first pass. This time, I have my notebook right next to the laptop, and I read all the way through it before each chapter.

As I'm in the chapter, I can fix the big issues. Sometimes they are just minor things. Other times, the block edit becomes a complete rewrite. I also save a new file called "seconddraft" before starting. I keep all of my first drafts for reference, and generally start a new file before each editing pass.

"Blocks" can be paragraphs, sentences, scenes, or whole chapters. I move everything around so that it flows better. Then I do another read-through, repeat the block edit if necessary, and when I'm happy, I move to the next phase.

Cleanup Edit

This is probably what most people think of when it comes to editing a novel. I'm looking at things like grammar, syntax, word choice, repeated nouns and verbs, dialogue tags, etc. My red pen is furious on this pass, and I will often print the whole manuscript and paint it with oxblood (my favorite editing ink).

I hunt down and destroy adjectives and helper words. I smite every use of the following words: had, just, almost, was, ready, starting, about, that, and any word ending in -ly. You might notice some of these words appear in this book. Non-fiction is very different than a novel.

I hunt for telly writing, and expand it into prose. I take overly flowery prose and condense it to eliminate the fluff. If I can't figure out what to do with an annoying sentence, I kill it. I cut paragraphs and scenes, and sometimes whole chapters. I'll even remove or add characters.

I'm also typically getting bored with the story at this point, so I start weaving in new side plots as I tighten things up. If a story is a Persian rug, then the first draft is the loom. Editing is where the magic happens. This is where you come up with all those added bits of intrigue that make your story deeper and more profound. I realized while writing Viral Spark, that the reason movies and books have such wonderful little twists and easter eggs isn't because the author planned them. She got bored, and started weaving details together. Depending on the author this may have been done in any phase of the writing process, but it was most definitely the result of repetitive iteration. At least that's my theory.

While I used to think of this pass as monotonous, I quite enjoy it now. Picking out all the prickly little details. Each word pleading it's desire to exist in my book. Every fanciful sentence that dies in a splash of red ink is confined forever to the hard drive, where it will never again catch a human eye. It's fun.

Rinse, Repeat

I go back to the beginning. I start over again at page one, with my notebook, and do the whole thing over. When I'm editing, I refuse to spend more than five minutes picking at a sentence, because I know I'll scan over it again, and I'll have another crack at it. I lose count of how many revisions I've gone through. I come up with clever names for files, like revision number, draft number, alpha, beta, gamma, final draft, final polish, etc. Faster editing equals more passes, which equals better overall product.

Typo Hunts

You want to talk about boring? This is it. Typo hunts will make you cross-eyed. Because of that, I like to reduce the number of passes I make in this phase by doing weird things.

I read the script backwards. I start at the last sentence, and work my way through the manuscript, one sentence at a time, looking for errors. This works because your brain can't process the story and distract you.

Read it out loud. There is no faster way to find mistakes then hearing the pacing and rhythm of the words, the way a sentence hits your brain. You limit yourself to around 300 words per minute, which does wonderful things to the editing process. You will begin picking up on things that you never noticed before.

If you want to make this technique even more effective, this is what you do. Turn on a tape recorder, or a voice recorder app on your phone, and record the audible version of your book. You will catch everything.

Once you have gone through this whole process, then your story is done. When editing passes contribute nothing but shifting a comma here or there, then you know it's ready. I'll admit it. I'm a little lazy with this sometimes, but I know that another editor is going to find a bunch of things for me to fix anyway, so I don't sweat it too much. If you are wondering when to squeeze in beta reviews for reader feedback, I usually do that after the block edits and a cleanup.

It's not easy. It's a time-consuming pain in the butt that will leave you wondering why you started writing that damn book. But it's worth it in the end. Trust me. Edit until your eyes cross and your fingers bleed, and then edit some more.

Roads are made of broken rocks.

-Martin McConnell

Chapter Twelve

Query Letter Hell

The scariest thing you will ever have to do as an author is send out a query letter. You thought beta reviews were rough? Ha! You ain't seen nothing yet.

It's one thing to send a copy of your book off to a friend, and ask for their honest opinion (if you can manage to squeeze it out of them), but sending your book off to a professional will keep you up at night, sometimes for weeks. Waiting, wondering.

"Did they get my letter?"

"If I call them and ask, will they find it, and toss it in the trash?"

"Will I hear back from them at all?"

The reason that this process is such a brain drain is quite simple. You are asking someone who represents books for a living if your baby is good enough. Their opinion, as an industry expert, matters. Couple that with waiting six to eight weeks for a reply, and you have a recipe for the most frustrating two months of your life.

First off, don't worry. I'm here to help you with your query, or at least guide you to the right sources for further advice that will stay more current than this text. Second, this is part of the process, and we've all gone through it, so suck it up. Third, one agent's opinion of your book doesn't add up to a ham sandwich. Be ready for criticism, and embrace it.

When I send out queries, I don't do it like a scared writer. I do it like a business professional. I start with a spreadsheet of all the agents that I believe can represent my work properly, and who don't have personality quirks that conflict with my own. I check back on the status after the allotted time-frame, or simply move on to the next agent on the list. If they don't have time to write me a response, then I don't have time to go chasing after them. This is a business. Treat it like one.

Over the last ten years, I've gotten several manuscript requests. As of this writing, I haven't wowed any agents with my stories, though I have gotten some good feedback that helped to shape me as an author. I saw what worked, and though it's different for every agent, I'll give you the steps to working through this process.

Don't Spam Agents, Make a List

Probably the biggest mistake you can make, is to send a form query letter out to 200 agents and see who bites. It's unprofessional and lazy, and all you will get back is form replies.

Agents, remember, are real people with real feelings. They sometimes get 100-200 queries or more a week. How does that make you feel about your personal inbox? You think an agent is going to be excited when she sees a query addressed to "Dear Sir or Madam?"

Start the process right by screening every agent you intend to query. Look them up on social media. Google their name and look at blogs written by people who have worked with them. Look at what kind of books they represent. If the books they are into are nothing like yours, then pass, and save both of you the time.

Keep only the best agents for your book on the list. The ones that you like personally, and who represent work like yours. Consider future works (like that next novel coming down the pipe), and if the agent would be a good fit for those also. Be picky, and find only the right agents for your book.

On your list, write down their submission requirements, their contact information, and which agency they work for.

Tighten up that Query Letter

You don't want to send this:

Dear Jean Paul Agent Dude,

I just finished my book, it's 80,000 words, and I think you would be a perfect fit.

CINDY LYNN finds herself in the middle of a love triangle between two of her closest friends. Things get heated, and she has a decision to make.

Ask yourself the following question. Does the above query tell you *anything* about the story at all? Why is she in a love triangle? Is that something she does as a hobby? Why and when do things get heated? What decision? What is this story even about? Who is this Cindy Lynn person? What's her deal? You might be chuckling, or think that I'm exaggerating on this point. I assure you, I am not.

I've read over a hundred query letters on AbsoluteWrite. The first draft of a query is usually so vague that you wouldn't be able to tell if it was closer to Star Wars or Harry Potter. Vague is bad, okay?

The elements that every query letter needs haven't changed much. You need to have your word count on there, rounded to the nearest thousand or so. You need to have the main characters name, and the little synopsis should follow the voice of the story. You need to clarify, in as few words as possible, who the main character is, what they want, and what the stakes are. And if you have any writing credits, you should list those, too.

I've found that it's a good idea to also toss in a sentence (ONE sentence) directed at the agent. Think of this as a way to show them that you actually did your homework when you selected them, and you didn't just pull their name out of an agent source book. And don't say "I just finished my book." Any query with those words goes straight in the trash. Oh yea, for fuck sake, spell their name right.

Test Your Query Letter

There are a couple of sites for this. Queryshark.blogspot.com is a good place to read some sample queries, though I think it's gone inactive. Also, if you don't have an AbsoluteWrite account, then get one. After a certain number of posts, you can submit your query to their *Query Letter Hell* forum, where other authors can help you. You can also help others with their query letters.

I know it sounds silly, but even if you don't have a clue what you are doing, help other people with their query letters. Think of yourself as a beta reader. The result is that you will become an expert on what a good query letter looks like in no time. I named this chapter after that forum subtitle for a reason. The critters have sharp teeth, but they will help you draft a much cleaner query letter with a better chance of getting an agent's attention.

Follow Instructions

To the letter. Figure out what they want, and give it to them. Don't sneak in extra pages, or try to skirt their system. All you are going to do is annoy them. If they say five pages, send them five double-spaced pages, starting at page one. Font twelve, TNR or Courier. Don't try to be fancy, because you aren't going to impress anyone.

Also, try not to query more than two or three agents at a time. Remember, the road to publication is slow, so don't rush it. And after you send it off, mark the date on your calendar, however many weeks out they said they would answer, and get on with your life.

Don't wait around for months on your query letters to come back. Keep writing. Keep working on your next story, your blog, your social platforms, or whatever else. You're an author now, and querying is a administrative thing. It shouldn't stop you from being creative and writing stories.

When that query response does come back, ignore it until the afternoon sometime, when you've finished your writing. Pour a glass of your favorite beverage, and open it will the full expectation to see a form rejection. It might help to have the next query submission ready to go before you open the letter, just as a mental reinforcement.

To gain your own voice, you have to forget about having it heard.

-Allen Ginsberg

Chapter Thirteen

Don't be an Aspiring Author

I didn't realize it for the longest time. It wasn't until after I started my full-time writing gig, actually, that one of the most crippling ways to reinforce self-doubt, is by calling yourself and aspiring-author, or an aspiring-anything for that matter.

Like any modifying adjective (I mentioned in one of the previous chapters that those should be cut from your prose), when you call yourself "aspiring," you are subconsciously acknow-ledging the fact that you aren't good enough to be the noun that follows. So forget the word *aspiring* altogether.

I learned this lesson in a rather odd way. I was out looking for freelancing gigs, and a friend (who earns money on her words) told to drop the freelancing BS. She said that title attracts clients who want to use you without providing adequate compensation for your services.

"Aspiring" is even worse. It puts a mental barrier between who you are now and who you want to be. Do yourself a favor. If you are writing, then call yourself a writer. Writing a book? Call yourself an author. Finished a novel? Novelist. It's that simple.

I can already hear the groaning of the old guard, who have, in their mind, given each of these terms a special meaning, and will criticize me for my classification. Here's the funny thing about writers. Most of us live in our little writing den, cut off from the rest of the world. Like every other human, we've created a make-believe version of the world in our minds. We see the universe how we want to.

The fucked up part about writers, due to our reclusive nature, is that there's nobody there to really argue with our perception. We converse online with people like us, who generally agree with us. Our audience generally agrees with us. This is where I break the status quo.

I'm not part of that life. I have friends who are Democrats, and others who are Republicans. I know chronic drug users and straight arrows. I've seen a lot of shit that I don't even want to comment on.

That's not to say that I'm special in this regard, far from it. We've each seen the dark side of life in one facet or another. As I dig deep into conversations with people, I realize that their world view, like mine, is shaped by both the good and bad aspects of society.

I see so many people though, especially in the writing community, that seek to criticize that which is irrelevant to the writing process. While I would have no trouble coming up with more of these sticking points, the only one relevant to this chapter is the nomenclature that we use to describe ourselves and others.

There seems to be two camps. Those who toss words like writer, artist, musician, author, and even bestseller around without constraint, and those who seek to constrain these words to very specific qualifiers. Some even going so far as to say if you aren't getting paid to write, you aren't a writer.

It's probably easy to see which camp I fall into. And while I don't agree with everyone, even on my side of the argument, I do think that the specific labeling of writers into different categories based on their social status or paycheck is fucking petty. Write is a verb, therefore, a person who writes gets the suffix. If you write, then you are a writer.

It doesn't matter how many books you've sold, how much money your words make, or who publishes them. It doesn't matter if they are published at all. It boils down, in my mind, to a simple distinction. If writing is what you want to do, and if you are writing to that end, if you create, then you can call yourself a writer, and fuck anyone who criticizes you for doing so. They aren't helping you, and they probably aren't helping themselves by wasting time explaining their definition of *writer* instead of, oh I dunno, writing?!

Nomenclature and semantics are stupid things to argue about (another point many writers will disagree with). Languages evolve, they change over time. I dare say that modern Italian is nothing like Roman Latin. And for that matter, anyone who thinks they know the best way to pronounce Latin words is just kidding themselves.

Writing is very much an artistic endeavor. And like all such pursuits, motivation is incredibly important. Maintaining your drive forward is a necessity. I can't spit out 10,000 words in a day because I'm especially gifted, but I've learned what kind of encouragement I need, that works for me, and I use that encouragement to meet my daily goals. On those rare days when I do hit 10,000, I'm both ecstatic and humbled.

The happiness comes from knowing that I gave it everything that day. I hit that mental barrier. I fought the monster of writer's block, and I won.

The humility comes from knowing other authors who have set the bar higher, and can get 20,000 when they push it.

The most important part of writing isn't the word count. The important part of any artistic pursuit isn't the bragging rights of a gallery exhibit, or a six-figure advance check on a book. It's being who you are, and doing that thing that you love so much, even when your mind, your friends, your family, and life are telling you otherwise.

If you are pushing hard, doing what you love, at all costs, and pursuing writing with a passion, then call yourself a writer, or a poet, or an author. Don't listen to the people telling you what you aren't yet. Be who you are, and start right now.

I've stressed, time and again through this work, that the secret to overcoming blocks, and finishing the damn book, is attitude. Here we are, full circle. If there is one thing, just one, that you take from what you've read, let it be this. Stop aspiring, start being, and own that shit.

Thanks for reading. I'm going to leave you with my all-time favorite quote ever.

I firmly believe that any man's finest hour,

the greatest fulfillment of all that he holds dear,

is that moment when he has worked his heart out in a good cause

and lies exhausted on the field of battle

– victorious.

-Vince Lombardi

Afterward

When I started writing this book, I knew that I wanted it to be much more than a book. I want it to spread. I want every writer out there who is having trouble finding their groove to have a source they could go back to. I want them all to finish their books. So I'm giving chapters 1-7 away for free, as a PDF.

If you know a writer who you think could benefit from this book, send them over to:

www.writefarmlive.com/coupon

The first seven chapters are right there for download. You don't have to do anything, you don't have to give me your email address. You don't have to sign up for a promotion, just download the booklet. This afterward is included in that book too. Tell your friends.

I plan on using this page in the future for more promotional goodies, so by the time you read this, it might be loaded with discount links or other free stuff. Check it out when you get a chance.

If you loved this book, and you would like to help spread the word about it's benefits, email me at spottedgeckgo@gmail.com, see what I'm up to, and how you can help. If you're a blogger and want to interview me or write a post about the book, email me and tell me about it. If you want to stay posted on revisions, updates, and special promotions, let me know that too. I'll let you know what I'm doing with the book, and when and where it's going down.

Most of all, I hope you enjoyed the book. Electronic books can be revised, updated, and made better. That's why I made this an e-book to begin with. If there's something I can do to make it better, let me know about it. Email me at spottedgeckgo@gmail.com, or use the Google form, there's a link on:

www.writefarmlive.com/coupon

At the end of the day, I want you to finish your damn book. Thanks so much for reading, there's some more goodies in the appendices. But don't waste too much time. Get writing!

Appendix A

Inspirational Quotes

My favorite quotes that encourage me to start my day, or sit down and get to work. I keep all of these in a special notebook that stays with my laptop, in case I need a boost of encouragement. I'm sharing the best ones with you. I hope they stir the same encouragement for you. Some are sayings that I've made up over the years.

He who would learn to fly one day must first learn to stand and walk and run and climb and dance; one cannot fly into flying.

-Friedrich Nietzsche

Writing doesn't just communicate ideas; it generates them.

-Paul Graham

Optimism is a perfectly legitimate response to failure.

-Stephen King

Success is achieved by developing our strengths, not by eliminating our weaknesses.

-Marilyn vos Savant

There is nothing to writing. All you do is sit down at the typewriter and bleed.

-Ernest Hemingway

Failure is as much a part of life as breathing.

-Martin McConnell

Prose is architecture, not interior decoration.

-Ernest Hemingway

I love deadlines. I like the wooshing sound they make as they fly by.

-Douglas Adams

Inaction breeds doubt and fear. Action breeds confidence and courage.

-Dale Carnegie

I scrape a little, sir. I torment a fiddle from time to time.

-Patrick O'Brian

Come in or out, there's a good fellow. Don't stand in the door like a Goddamned Lenten cock.

-Patrick O'Brian

A one-page breakthrough starts an avalanche.

-Nancy K. Haddock

You must stay drunk on writing so reality cannot destroy you.

-Ray Bradbury

Men strike out their permanent characters; or have those characters struck into them.

-Patrick O'Brian

This is how you do it: you sit down and you put one word after another until it's done. It's that easy, and that hard.

-Neil Gaiman

Blessed are the meek, for they shall inherit the earth.

-Matthew 5:5

When you write an exhilarating scene, it leaves a mark on you.

-Martin McConnell

The difference between fiction and reality?
Fiction has to make sense.

-Tom Clancy

Focus on where you want to go, not on what you
fear.

-Anthony Robbins

To gain your own voice, you have to forget about
having it heard.

-Allen Ginsberg

If you don't have time to read, you don't have
the time (or the tools) to write.

-Steven King

Nodding the head does not row the boat.

-Irish Proverb

If you really want to do something you'll find a way, if you don't you'll find an excuse.

-Jim Rohn

A person who never made a mistake never tried anything new.

-Albert Einstein

Roads are made of broken rocks.

-Martin McConnell

By failing to prepare, you are preparing to fail.

-Benjamin Franklin

If you wait for inspiration to write; you're not a writer, you're a waiter.

-Dan Poynter

A superior man is modest in his speech, but exceeds in his actions.

-Confucious

I may not have gone where I intended to go, but I think I have ended up where I needed to be.

-Douglas Adams

Writing is most of all an exercise in determination.

-Tom Clancy

Mother nature will get the last laugh. That bitch will take everything.

-John McConnell

The first draft of anything is shit.

-Ernest Hemingway

Start before you are ready.

-Steven Pressfield

A professional writer is an amateur who didn't quit.

-Richard Bach

Start where you are. Use what you have. Do what you can.

-Arthur Ashe

Don't succumb to excuses. Go back to the job of making the corrections and forming the habits that will make your goal possible.

-Vince Lombardi

Appendix B

Recommended Reading

I'm not going to church it up with a bunch of MBA formatted bullshit. We live in the the digital age, for Pete's sake, and this isn't a reference list for the book. It is a list of books written by much more talented authors than I, which will help you on your writing journey. I wasn't paid for any of these endorsements, some came highly recommended from my advance readers.

The Artist's Way by Julia Cameron

The Art of War by Steven Pressfield

5000 Words Per Hour: Write Faster, Write Smarter by Chris Fox

Creative Writing Cancer: Becoming a Writer of · Film, Video Games, and Books by Justin M. Sloan

Do the Work by Steven Pressfield

Growth Hacker Marketing by Ryan Holiday

The Motivation Manifesto by Brendon Burchard

Lessons From a Lifetime of Writing by David Morrell

Life's Golden Ticket: A Story About Second Chances by Brendon Burchard

On Writing by Stephen King

The Pocket Muse by Monica Wood

The Secret by Rhonda Byrne

Structuring Your Novel Workbook: Hands-On Help for Building Strong and Successful Stories by K.M. Weiland

This Year You Write Your Novel by Walter Mosley

Who moved my cheese? by Spencer Johnson

The Writer's Block Myth: A Guide to Get Past Stuck & Experience Lasting Creative Freedom by Heloise Jones

A Year of Writing Dangerously: 365 Days of Inspiration and Encouragement by Barbara Abercrombie

Appendix C

Kick-Ass Writing Websites

www.absolutewrite.com

www.writersdigest.com

www.writefarmlive.com ←yep, plugged it :P

www.victoriagriffin.net

www.thewritelife.com

www.helpingwritersbecomeauthors.com

www.quickanddirtytips.com

www.creativewritingprompts.com

www.writingforums.org

Appendix D

Story Submission Format

Full Name   about 300 words
Address 1   Story Genre
Town, ST 00001
Phone Number
Email@address.com

        Title Halfway Down the Page

              by Full Name

    Indent every paragraph, and use a
normal font like Courier or Times New
Roman. If using Courier, anything you
want italicized should be underlined.
You should also double-space your
lines. I'm not doing that here to save
page space. Set the font size to 12.

This makes your script easier to read by the editor, and the line spacing allows them to make notes on a printed document. Don't use colored paper or fancy borders. Black lettering, white paper, this should go without saying, but… Oh yeah, and only print on one side of the page.

You might notice the header on this page. Start page numbers on page 2, and leave the header right-aligned on the page. These should be in the top right corner of every single page, in case the editor wants to put a staple on the left corner. You can shorten your title to a word or two (usually the last word), and only use your last name.

The by-line should be one double-space below the title. The margins an inch on each side of an 8-1/2 by 11 inch paper.

LastName / TitleKeywords / 3

Use two hyphens to indicate an M-dash--just like this--especially if using a courier font, and mark line breaks with a single, centered hash-tag like this.

#

For longer manuscripts, like novel submissions, I generally leave the title page for title and contact information, and start my novel on the following page.

These are general guidelines that most publishers, magazines, and agents will be happy with, but always check their specific submission guidelines and make adjustments as needed. Online magazines will sometimes want the submission free of indentation, because it's easier to move the text to a website. Sometimes italics are allowed (especially for submission in TNR) but not always.

LastName / TitleKeywords / 4

Hopefully, this little snippet will help you with basic formatting and submission block-up.

Appendix E

Writer's Glossary

Adjective – A word that must fight for its right to exist in a book.

Advance – Money that you get upfront for selling first publishing rights to a publisher.

Appendix – This thing in your belly.

Aspiring – A word that should be stripped from your title, your writing, and probably the English language. It serves no purpose but to crush motivation.

Author – Someone who writes books.

Bedtime – The time between writing and waking up.

Book proposal – This is like a query letter, but specifically for publishers.

Critique – Cry about it all you want, but this is something your book needs to get better. A critter claws and chews through your manuscript looking for errors.

Coffee – A creative fuel that can be used to generate books.

Contract – Find a good lawyer.

Dedication – A good time to offer either praise or revenge, depending on your goals.

Draft – The first piece of shit that you crank out to kick off the writing process.

Editor – Someone who points out everything you are doing wrong, so you can fix it. Editors come in many different flavors. Taste the rainbow.

Fiction – Truf.

First Draft – The first iteration of the story writing process. Finish it fast, so you can start revisions and edits.

Genre – A nonspecific classification scheme designed so that booksellers can figure out where to put things on a shelf.

Glossary – A list of definitions that differs from the standard Oxford Dictionary.

Influencer – A person or group who inspires another person or group to action, for bad, for good, or for awesome.

Line Edit – A comprehensive finishing stage of the editing process, where the manuscript is scoured for things like spelling errors, shitty grammar, flow, and sequencing.

Literary Agent – The gatekeepers of the traditional publishing world. Literary agents will pitch your book to publishers, and advise you on your budding writing career. They aren't half as evil as people make out.

Manuscript – Your novel, as it is when you submit it for publication or review.

Midlist – Authors who got that awesome novel contract, but never made it very far afterward.

Monster – A fictional creature in your mind that stops you from doing the thing you set out to do.

Muse – A Greek goddess who inspires with her kisses.

Non-fiction – Lies and blasphemy.

Novelist – Someone who writes novels, or has written a novel.

Poetry – A group of words that sound pretty when read. They have a beat and a tempo, carefully crafted, in order to convey an emotion in both meaning and sound.

Proof Copies – Your last chance to check the book for potential fuck-ups.

Prose – Words you are proud of.

Publicist – Someone who actually knows how to talk to media people. Will probably be your best friend, if you are lucky enough to have one.

Publisher – Anyone who distributes or makes public documents or files. This can be a blogger, a book publisher, or yourself. If you "publish" anything, then you are a publisher.

Query Letter – A letter of intent, usually short, that asks permission to submit a story or guest blog to a publisher. This could be a request to an agent to look at your novel, a request to a blogger for an interview or guest post, or a request from the agency to the publisher.

Reading Fees – A fee that dip-shit companies charge you to have the honor of letting them decide if your book or short story is good enough.

Returns – This is fucked up. No other business does this except the book business. When a book store decides after six months that your book isn't selling enough, they can send it back for a refund.

Revisions – Where real writers live.

Royalties – Money that you get from actual sale of copies of your finished book, though in many cases, "actual sales" is open to interpretation.

Slush Pile – A stack of incoming paperwork that must be sifted through, to separate the gems from the garbage.

Target Audience – The people out there in the world who would actually be willing to buy your book, if marketed to properly.

Writer – Someone who writes.

Writer's Block – A lie told to budding authors to keep them from finishing their book. Anti-motivation. The monster. Opposite of muse.

About the Author

Martin McConnell has a degree in Physics, writes non-stop, and is currently earning a living on his words. He's been in and around the novel writing community for over 10 years, has a stockpile of unfinished and mostly finished works, a passion for space and fast cars, and brings his writing shit with him to parties and bars.

You can find him anywhere on social media, though he usually lives online through his alter ego, @spottedgeckgo on Twitter. You can write him an email at spottedgeckgo@gmail.com, or find his website at www.writefarmlive.com for all the writing tips you will ever need.

Every good story has a main character who drives the plot. Own your story, and drive your own plot.

Printed in Great Britain
by Amazon